Engaging Parents

Lamar Collins

authorHOUSE®

AuthorHouse™
1663 Liberty Drive
Bloomington, IN 47403
www.authorhouse.com
Phone: 1-800-839-8640

First published by AuthorHouse 4/30/2010

ISBN: 978-1-4490-1710-1 (e)
ISBN: 978-1-4490-1709-5 (sc)

Printed in the United States of America
Bloomington, Indiana

This book is printed on acid-free paper.

Contents

About Lamar (Coach) Collins

Lamar (Coach) Collins grew up in an at risk environment as the product of a single parent home. Upon graduation he enlisted in the U.S. Army. While in the Army he met several key individuals that led him on the path to manhood. He decided to get out of the Army after one tour (although he did 11 more years in the U.S. Army Reserves) to pursue a career in teaching. After graduating from Central Texas College and the University of Mary-Hardin Baylor, Lamar taught in the Killeen ISD. After four years of teaching (PE and Science) and coaching (football, basketball, and track) he was asked to join and effort of Scott and White Healthcare to attack the unfortunate rise of teenage pregnancies in Bell county Texas. While working for Scott and White Healthcare, Lamar travelled across the country, speaking to physician groups, educators, students and non profit and governmental agencies. When the grant he worked under expired, he took a job within the hospital, but began getting calls from around the country to conduct student assemblies and staff development. He started the Collins Education Group (www.collinseducationgroup.org) and is now a much requested speaker and fundraiser across the country.

Chapter 1: What's the Goal?

If your school or organization is like most, you've found that those you'd really like to reach, are the least likely to come to your event. Oftentimes, there is tremendous excitement about the effects that will follow your planned event. Unfortunately, this is usually followed up with a let down over the amount of parental/adult participants. Weeks and sometimes months spent preparing for an event, ensuring everything is in place is met with a response of 15 parents (if you're lucky). A location that could hold hundreds was used for only a handful of attendees. To make matters worse, the ones that came are the ones already on board, supporting the message. The group that you really set out to reach didn't even show up. We have not even considered the amount of money spent on pizza, chips, cookies, door prizes, etc. If this illustration describes your efforts, I've written this to help you increase the effectiveness of your outreach.

The goal of most events is to help the parents of the children struggling academically or behaviorally, through seminars and/or literature. While that is an honorable (and needed) goal, for the most part it's an ineffective approach if you want them to come. The words seminar and literature to some parents are a huge turn off. Think about it, you are **saying** your event is a parent training or a parent outreach. But some **are hearing** you say that they are **unfit parents** so come to this event so that we can help you understand what you are doing wrong. While some parents understand the importance of continually growing and getting new ideas to better serve their children; others look at your program as an insult-- especially the at risk parents (I do not use this as a term of disrespect, but as a way to identify the parents of children that are most likely to engage in risky behavior), which is who you are really trying to reach. Also, realize that many of the parents that you want to reach (the at risk parents) do want to better serve their children; however, coming to your event is almost an admission that they are not good parents. Some of you may have even encountered opposition when you invited them to your event. If we want to reach them, it is important that we **give them what they want**, not **what we want them to have** (even though it is what they need). There is an old saying that you attract more flies with honey than with vinegar. In keeping with this analogy, I want to suggest that you attract more parents with fun than you do with a preachy message of what they are doing wrong, and why they need to listen to you because you have the answers. Oftentimes, when they see you, they take one look at you and say how in the world could this person help me with my child. And quite honestly, they are justified in their thinking. What makes you think that you can help them with their children, when you don't understand their culture (whether this is true or not, it is their perception, which makes it their reality)? Your view of what they need may be taken as an insult. So now the question becomes how do I help them, when they take my help as an insult? The answer is not as difficult as it may seem. Approach the issue a different way. Instead of primarily focusing on giving them what you want them to have (which is what they need), focus on giving them what they want. What do they want? I'm glad asked. Before I go on, let me again stress that fact that many parents really do want to be better parents, but they weren't parented good, and never received parenting training. Some are actually doing the best they can; they just don't know any better. There are even some that would like to come to your event, but after working

8-10 hours, coming home just to go back to work (cooking dinner, checking homework, household chores—you guys know what I'm talking about), they just can't seem to find the time or the energy to go to your event.

What do parents want?

Parents want their children to be happy, and this is what we must make our goal. Let's focus on developing a program that the children will want to come attend with their parents. To do this we spend the majority of the time on what they want and give a 10-15 minute sound bite of what they need. Let's go a little further, instead of saying that we are having a parent education night, say that we are having a **family fun night**. Let them know that on this night we will offer extra credit or homework passes (if your school allows it). Also let them know that we will be playing volleyball, dodge ball (students vs the teachers and parents) and board games for the adults and students that would rather not be active. It may sound a little careless to hold an event that we only allocate 10-15 minutes to actual parent developing, but I can't stress how important this format is. Let me also suggest that the verbal presentation is only 10-15 minutes, but the actual "teaching" is going on all night. It is my firm belief that some things can't be taught, they must be caught. I developed this philosophy from a lecture I was in. The lecturer said that we must train children in the right way and I felt like the light bulb went on. You see, to teach is to tell, but to train is to show. When I teach a child, I talk about appropriate behavior. When I train a child, I model appropriate behavior. The family fun night is designed to model appropriate behavior to both the students and the parents. Take respect for example. Respect is something that is caught not taught. I can't teach you to be respectful. You learn respect when you see someone you admire acting respectful. In doing so, you learn to keep you cool, when you really feel like going off. Our kids are the same way. If appropriate behavior has rarely been modeled to them, it's too easy to display the negative behavior they've grown accustomed to. We must get them in a non-threatening environment and allow them to see us acting respectful. We are also showing the parents how to respect their children. Guys as I've traveled across Central Texas doing this, I've found it quite therapeutic. It's amazing what can happen in a short 1 ½ meeting. I'm getting excited just thinking about it! Let's get back to the actual program.

By focusing on the "fun", you get the students, parents, and even some teachers' attention. Students nor parent want to come to hear how bad or good things are, but the same parents that couldn't get off of work and were just too tired to make it to school events will find themselves energized and off for this occasion. You now have parents attending that would have never attended your boring parent meeting (don't take it so personal).

A little more

The family fun night will give them the message you want them to have, it just won't give them the entire message in one setting. We will promote the fun and have a blurp of the message. I know, some of you are saying that we have to give them more substance to justify the expense. To that, I ask which you would rather have, and event with 15 parents that could give your presentation or 150 parents who really need your presentation given one of your points. I want to suggest that getting a little of the message is better than getting none of it. Give it to them in bite size chunks and at the same time, develop healthy relationships between parents, teachers, and students is quite an accomplishment. Remember, we are not just teaching, we are training. When we play games with the kids, encouraging, respecting, and treating them correctly, we are modeling the appropriate behavior to parents on how to treat their children. How awesome is that. Listen, I'm not saying after one event the parents are going to become better parents, but after a couple of events, they will eventually get it. We must remember, we are not in a sprint, this is a marathon. The undesirable parents didn't get that way in one night and they won't be conformed in one night, but we have to start the process somewhere. Many of you have already started the process, let me help you continue to challenge the parents to change in a non-threatening way, by not just teaching them how to parent, but training them how to parent as they watch us interact with them and their children.

When I was a teacher, I remember asking for parent conferences just to see if my hunch was correct. When the parent came in acting irate, and blaming everyone for the child's problem, screaming all kinds of obscenities, I said to myself, yep that's exactly why the child acts like that. More attention children pay to what we do than what we say[1]. If we want children to act appropriately, they have to be modeled the appropriate action. If

---

1   I heard Zig Ziglar say this at one of his conferences

we want parents to act appropriately towards their children, then we must model the appropriate actions to them.

Competition is a perfect opportunity to model how we ought to treat each other. It's a perfect opportunity for them to see us respect their children and love their children, which is why I recommend a volleyball or dodgeball game. These subtle training moments over time can have a revolutionary effect. I know you want to see instant change, but remember, they didn't get to where they are in an instant, and they won't get out in an instance. This process is a marathon, not a sprint.

Finally, I think 1 ½ hours is enough time to put on a good event. It's at this time that you begin to loose people. We'll talk about the program a little later, but keep this time frame in mind. I don't include the activity in the event. Appendix A shows a template of a successful family fun night.

Chapter 2: Marketing

You have the idea, but that's only the beginning. Now we have to work the idea. Let's get people excited about getting the word out. We have to let everyone know what we are doing and stress how much fun (notice we are stressing the fun, not the presentation) they are going to have. Marketing has to be different that in the past. I know, previously your marketing has been to put an ad in the paper and a PSA (public service announcement) on the radio (the Christian radio station). Unfortunately this doesn't work. The parents you need to reach (typically) don't read the paper and they (typically) don't listen to those stations. A better idea would be to simply go into Microsoft powerpoint, and develop a flyer of students having fun. Place these flyers around the school for all to see. Be sure to place flyers in the office, cafeteria, gymnasium, and at all of the entrances to the school. If you can schedule the event around a date where the school sends a major mail out to all parents, have a blurb on the mail out promoting the event. If your school/organization has a website, it's also important to put your event on the website. Another marketing method is to use the morning announcements to your advantage. Have a very popular teacher or administrator (this could be one that is really liked or one that is really disliked) and a very popular student talk about the event. For example, have the teacher talk about how he/she is looking forward to beating the students in volleyball, or getting all of the students out in dodge ball, or explaining why no one can beat him in checkers. Then have a student come back and talk about how the students plan to beat the "old people". This will generate tremendous excitement. Everyone will want to be a part of this event. If you could get an administrator involved that would be good also. You may even have to charge! It would also do you well to inform the area churches that the school is trying to help develop parent-child relationships. I've found it difficult to partner with churches, but you may have better success in your area.

Another key is to display prizes in strategic locations. For example, you want prizes in the cafeteria and in the office. These are high volume places that are sure to get people to asking questions. You want to have prizes in high volume areas with signs that say they will be given away on the date of your event. Buy the prizes and let the students see them. Another key marketing ploy is to use the school marquee. This is an opportunity to get the word out consistently. I suggest putting it in the marquee 3 weeks before the event. This will allow students to see it as they leave school and hopefully remember to say something to their parents. It will also remind them as the pass the marquee after school is out. This again can spur their memory when they are with their parents so that they will discuss what they have been hearing on the announcements.

Chapter 3: Freebie's

Freebies are also a must when it comes to attracting parents. Remember It's not what they need that will get them there, it's what they want. They want someone to feed their children; they want a babysitter for the toddlers, if only for a couple of hours (I think everyone that has toddlers can relate to needing break every now and then!). I know, some of you are thinking to yourself, we've tried that and it didn't work. I know it didn't work, but that's only because you didn't do it the right way. If you want it to work, you can't just do the right thing. You have to do the right thing the right way, and that's what this book is all about. Now let me tell you the right way of doing it. Get things the people you are trying to reach want. I've been places where the door prize was deer feed! Yes, deer feed. I didn't even know there was such a thing, but in that rural community it was a hit. Giving away tool kits, hunting gear, IPods or the like are all hits. Now here's the big key. You must buy the gifts at least two weeks before the event, and display them in the cafeteria and in the office. Not pictures of them, but the items themselves (if you can). Usually I recommend giving away a bike. Have the bike in the cafeteria for all of the students to see. If you have a display case, have the janitors put the IPod (example) in the display case with a sign saying it will be given away on a given night. Put the DVD player in the lunch line by the check out lady in the cafeteria with a sign say who is going to win me. If you can't put the actual item there, then pictures will do, but if you can, use the item itself. This will create an interest and people will come. They won't come for your program, they'll come for your freebies, but as long as they are there, who cares why! Look in the marketing chapter on how to successfully market your freebies. Another good thing to give away would be a homework pass for all attendees that bring a parent or older brother or sister (remember older sibling have tremendous influence over younger siblings). Some school districts don't allow this, but many do. If yours does, I'll assure you that this will get parents out there. Post this in the office, letting parents that come in for conferences or signing their students in/out know that there will be an opportunity to get a free 100% homework grade will greatly appeal to them. As teachers, we all know that one 100% in homework will not really make a huge difference over the course of a semester, but it works. Since it works and it's something they want, use it. It would be good to try to get other organizations involved. Many locally owned businesses in your area would love to show their support to schools. Ask them to put flyers in their window and while you're at it, ask them to sponsor and item for give-away. There is always a pizza place, local businessperson, or other entity that will donate gifts and food. Speaking of food, I've found pizza is a can't loose. If you're like me, you're not really interested in eating pizza, but kids love it, and when it's free, parents love it. Pizza is also typically easy to get. The hard part is trying to gauge how much to order. I've seen some real catastrophe's occur when schools over order, but even bigger catastrophes when they under order. You'd be surprised how people act over a slice of pizza. I haven't found a specific way to actually fix this (if you think of one email me), but a gauge could be to have homeroom teachers give out and receive participation slips. Quarter sheets of paper, talking about the event, especially what will be given away, and have them signed and returned by a significant adult in their life. Of course this doesn't mean that more will not show up, nor does it mean that all that signed will show up, but it does give you a barometer. And since it is pizza, you can let the manager of the local pizzeria know that you may be calling back for more pizza if things go better than expected.

Chapter 4: Showtime

Okay it's the day of the event. It's important to know that there will be surprises. It's very likely that some things may not go according to plan, but aren't you used to that by now. Don't get stressed out by minor set backs. However, I do want to tell you how to minimize the setbacks. First of all, we have to have a plan for the event. Make sure that the location of the event has enough tables, chairs, and trash cans to accommodate the expected audience. It would also be good to check the microphones at least 1 hour before the event. To check the microphones means that the janitors may need to know what we are planning. Let them know (at least 1 week in advance) that a microphone will be needed. It can work without a microphone, but it's been my experience that a good sound system makes things go so much better. Have sign in sheets prepared, a sample one[2] is provided (if you email me, I'll send you the excel spreadsheet). This is to show the success of the program. Many of you have been challenged by central office to get parental/community involvement, and this is a way to show you've done it (you know how it is, we have to document everything!). I would also appreciate you faxing me a copy of your sign in sheets showing me how successful it was. I love to hear success stories. You also must know the route the audience will travel. Where will they sign in? Where will the pizza be set up? Where should the trash cans be placed? These are all things that need to be considered before the people come. This should be set up approximately 45 minutes before the start of the

---

2　See appendix A

event. Remember, although the event starts at 6pm (for example) you can start expecting people around 5:30. You will need people to direct traffic. Instructing people to sign in, then go to the pizza line and the seated area. It can be a smooth sailing event, you can even have student volunteers. I don't recommend student volunteers to hand out the food unless you have some that you really trust, parents or teachers should probably be handling the food- with gloves.

For the event, a key to bringing in the people is to ask the choir to sing, a local group or cheerleaders to perform. The point is to get some entertainment. I've been to family fun nights with and without entertainment and both go well. I just think that when you have the students entertaining, it becomes another reason for parents, grandparent, aunts, uncles, and good friends to come. Again, a template of a model program is found in appendix A.

Chapter 5: Funding the Event

Funding the event is not as difficult as you may think. To fund the event, first let's develop a budget. Some of you are laughing, but seriously let's look at what we need. We need food. The amount of food needed will be difficult to determine because we do not have paid registration. When things are free, it's difficult to gauge how many will come. We talked about this a little in the marketing chapter, but let's explore it a bit further. The best way to do it may be to ask the students how many of them are bringing their parents. Start with enough food for about half of that number. I've seen this work well and I've seen it work not so well. What seems to work best is letting several pizza places know what you are doing and that you may need pizzas in a hurry. In rural areas, I've seen party subs ordered from local stores and I've even seen potlucks where the parents bring food. Some of you have policies that prevent that, but here is where you will have to decide what's best for you. Be advised, there are places that will donate to the school. Take advantage of this. They get a tax write off and recognition for partnering with a school to promote parental involvement. Let the business owner know that this is positive press for his/her business that can get written of at the end of the year. If this doesn't work, talk to the PTA/PTO's. They raise money for good causes and guess what, this is a good cause. They may actually be the ones you want to hand this off to and let them run with it. Listen, you as an administrator can't do it all and you don't have to do it all. There are very competent teachers on your staff and parent volunteers in your school, put them to work! And then praise them publicly for what they accomplish. If they need fundraising ideas, tell them to go to the local Rotary, Kiwanis, Lions clubs and other service organizations. These guys have money for the good of the community. Show them the good that you are doing. If this doesn't work, have a kiss the pig contest, where students give money in honor of a teacher they would like to see kiss the pig. Have a fundraising basketball or volleyball game and charge $0.50 per student to watch the game. When you start thinking you'd be amazed at the ideas you come up with. The point is that the funding does not have to come out your school's budget.

Chapter 6: The event

A good speaker is vital. If the speaker is not good, future events will loose credibility. I can not stress the importance of having someone that can connect with the audience. It may or may not be the principal, and that's okay. It may be a teacher, coach, a community leader, or someone brought in. If you do choose a professional/motivational speaker, I do have a suggestion—me. And yes, I will charge you. Whether you have someone on your staff or bring in a speaker, make sure they're good. I know that as the principal you'd like to be the one to address the parents, but this is not the time to let your ego get in the way. If you are not a good speaker, don't mess this up. On a side note if you bring in a speaker, it would be good to schedule student assemblies and/or staff developments during the same time, to get the most bang for your buck. It may even be good to partner with other schools in your area. The point is, get someone good.

Keep in mind, we have to have everyone in place and a flow established. They need to know where to sign in, where to go to get the food, where to sit down to eat, where to throw the food away, and how to transition from the cafeteria/auditorium, to the gym (or wherever you are having the games played). These minor details are very important, as they will ensure the program flows well and confusion is minimized.

Remember, I think the event should be scheduled for 1-11/2 hours. And yes, I still think you should only speak for approximately 15-20 minutes. I know it seems like a lot of resources for a 15-20 minute presentation, but let me reiterate, some things are caught not taught. There are things that children have to see modeled before they get it. I've said it before, but they have to see us respect others to learn to be respectful. That's why it is so important that throughout the event, school staff model the appropriate behavior. It is important that the parents in attendance see the staff being respectful to other staff, students, and parents. This is also a time when positive interactions can take place and relationships are developed. You do realize that students behave better in the classrooms of teachers the students' parents like, don't you? Developing these relationships will prove extremely valuable in the long run.

Chapter 7: Next Event

The success of this event will create excitement in the students, staff and family members involved. They will talk about it amongst themselves and others for months to come. Because of this free publicity, you will be getting, now would be a good time to let them know about your next event. This could be done by having a poster board by all of the exits, with the date of the next event. You can also direct the parents to your website, where you can have a blurp about your next event. Getting a date for your next event will put it in their minds and give them the opportunity to be your P.R. team. As others see and share their excitement about your events, attendance will likely rise. Again, I suggest doing these quarterly, giving parents a few nuggets each time; however, one or two are better than none. If you don't do events quarterly, take advantage of volleyball and basketball games, choir, orchestra and other UIL events. At halftime or intermission, remind parents of the "blurp". Appreciate them for coming and showing their support for their children. Then challenge them to read with their children, have their children explain what they are doing in math or some other activity that will build the parent/child relationship and promote academic success.

I think this will be also great opportunity to create parental involvement. Find a parent (or several) that are really enjoying themselves and ask them to help you with the next event. It would also be a great opportunity to give teachers with administrator aspirations administrative duties (thus developing them).

As you see, this is so much bigger than a simple parent outreach. It has become a parent training/ involvement, relationship building, and teacher development opportunity. Of course the students will benefit most, because as parents and staff develop relationships, the likelihood for referrals decrease, because of the relationship of the parent and school staff. Not to mention the fact that you are building the administrators of tomorrow. Please don't put this book down and say, "that's a good idea." Go ahead and call in one of your rising star teachers, have them get in contact with me, and let's make this happen!

Points to Remember

- The desires of the parents and the staff are the same

- Both want the same end, the question is the means to the end. It must be on their terms. Parents that need what you are offering aren't going to meet you on your terms. You must meet them on their terms;

- A well known/respected speaker always better

- Have popular teacher/coach/administrator talk the event up. Do not simply announce it, talk it up.

- Communication 55% body language, 38% tone and 7% word choice. This is why it is so important for parents to see how teacher carry themselves around students. The actual communication is the body language and tone that you use with children-- not the word choice.

- Have the event well organized. If this event goes well, parents are more apt to come to your next event.

- Enlist the help/participation of popular students/athletes. Let students that are popular and talk well talk it up also.

- When you ask for freebies from Wal-Mart, Sims, Kmart, Target, and others, always ask for more than you need for the event you're asking for, so that you can use the extra's for other events. This is called maximizing your contributions.

APPENDIX A

Before the Event

1. 1-3 month- have someone call possible donors
2. 1 month- ask choir or other group to perform
3. 3 weeks purchase give-aways and display in visible locations (also purchase raffle tickets for the give-aways)
4. 3 weeks- get commitment from student council/honor society to baby sit

5. 2 weeks- have daily announcements on the event, stressing the competitive events. Have a popular student and a popular teacher/administrator talk
6. 2 weeks- email/talk to coaches about using the gym. Talk to custodial staff about using the cafeteria and set up.
7. 2 weeks place posters around the campus
8. 1 week- call pizza/food places
9. 1 week- establish where sign in will be, where food will be served, where games will be played, and who will be responsible for each
   a. Sign in- 3 people
   b. Food- 4 people
   c. Games- at least 1 person per game location
10. Establish clean up crew

Day of event (start time 7pm)[3]

- Call to have pizza delivered

- 6:00pm- set up games and bring give aways into the cafeteria/designated location

- 6:00pm- Set up sign in area, feeding area, trash cans, and microphones

- 6:30pm- choir/performing group(s) should be in place

- 6:45pm- Begin sign in (unless crowd is large.. if so you may want to start sign in sooner). Give out raffle tickets and food

- 7pm- Intro to Family Fun Night and appreciate people for coming

---

3   If you start at a different time, simply change the bulleted times accordingly

- 7:05pm- Student groups perform while people are eating

- 7:20pm- Give ways (give away ½ of them now)

- 7:25pm- Speaker

- 7:40pm- Give away the other half now

- 7:45-8:30- play games and have fun!

After Thought

I'd like to personally thank all of my supporters, all of the organizations and schools I've been allowed to share my heart and passion with and most of all my wonderful family (Rose, Alexis, Alyssa, Aliyah, and TJ). I also want you to know that once I'm a part of your professional development, I take it personal, so if you ever have a question or comment please email me at coach@collinseducationgroup.org. I'd also be honored if you'd visit my website and leave a comment on the book (www.collinseducationgroup.org).